Imagine! 3

Oxford Read and Imagine

A Shadow on the Park

By Paul Shipton

Illustrated by Matteo Piana

Activities by Hannah Fish

Contents

Meet the Characters

Grandpa
Ben and Rosie's grandfather
Clunk
Grandpa's robot
Josh and Aunt Val
Ben and Rosie's little cousin, with his mom
Kelly
an architect
Ed
a teenager
Imagine!
Now enjoy this story, *A Shadow on the Park*.

Chapter One

'Can we go to the park?' said Josh. 'PLEASE!'

'Yes, OK,' said Grandpa. It was a beautiful summer afternoon, and he, Ben, and Rosie were in the city to see Aunt Val and their little cousin Josh.

'You can walk there in ten minutes,' said Aunt Val. 'Be good, Josh!'

When they were close to the park, Josh pointed. 'Wow! What's that?' he asked.

'It's a crane,' said Grandpa. 'Look. They're building a new tall building here.'

A lot of people were working on the new building.

→ Go to page 24 for activities.

Ben looked up at the new building. 'What's it going to be?'

A woman was walking by. She heard Ben's question. 'This building is going to be offices and apartments,' she said.

'It's going to be beautiful!' said Rosie.

‘Thanks. This building was my idea! I’m an architect,’ said the woman. ‘My name’s Kelly.’ She pointed across the park. ‘We’re building a second building there.’

Grandpa looked at the place for the second tall building. ‘Your buildings are going to be fantastic. But will they make a shadow on the park?’

Go to page 26 for activities.

Chapter Two

Josh was happy to be in the park, but soon he was cold.

'It's colder in this park,' said Grandpa. 'We're not in the sun now.'

'It's cold because we're in the shadow of the new building,' said Ben.

'Let's go to the playground!' said Clunk.

There were some teenagers at the playground. One of them was climbing on the slide.

'Come down, Ed!' said one of his friends.

Ed laughed. 'It's OK! I'm not going to fall. I love climbing!'

'Excuse me,' said Grandpa. 'You're too big for that slide.'

→ Go to page 28 for activities.

Ed laughed and jumped to the ground. He didn't say sorry.

'Come on,' Ed said to his friends. 'This place is boring.'

After Ed and his friends went, Ben and Rosie tried to play with Josh.

But their cousin was cold and tired now.

'I want to go home,' Josh said.

They started to leave the park, but suddenly Grandpa stopped. 'Listen!' he said.

They heard an angry shout: 'Hey! You can't climb up there!'

'That's Kelly!' said Grandpa. 'Come on!'

Ed's friends were there, but Ed wasn't with them.

Kelly was looking up at the crane and shouting.

Rosie looked up, too. 'Oh no!' she said.

Go to page 30 for activities.

Chapter Three

Ed was climbing up the crane.

He wasn't scared – he was having fun!

'Watch this!' he shouted down to his friends. 'I can climb anything!'

'Come down now!' shouted Kelly. 'You might fall!'

But Ed didn't listen to her. He went up and up.

Soon Ed was at the top of the crane. He put his hands up and started to laugh. 'Look at me up here!' he shouted.

Then he looked down. This crane was *very* high.

Ed stopped laughing. Now he was too scared to move. 'HELP!' he shouted.

Go to page 32 for activities.

'It's OK, Grandpa,' said Clunk. 'I can go up there and bring him down.'

The little robot started to climb up the crane.

'Be careful, Clunk!' said Ben.

The robot's body was heavy, but his arms were strong. He climbed up the crane fast.

When Clunk was at the top, he started to move across the arm of the crane.

'Please wait,' Clunk shouted to Ed. 'I'm coming to help you.'

Ed tried to hide it, but he was very scared. The wind was getting stronger and stronger …

Go to page 34 for activities.

Chapter Four

On the ground, Grandpa, Kelly, and the children were watching and waiting.

'Are they OK?' asked Rosie.

'I don't know,' said Grandpa. 'The sun's light is hitting Clunk's metal body and shining down, so I can't see!'

At the top of the crane, Clunk was getting closer to Ed.

'Give me your hand,' he said.

But suddenly, there was a very strong wind. Oh no! Ed started to fall.

'Help!' he shouted.

Now Ed was holding the crane with one hand.

'Please be quick!' he said to Clunk.

→ Go to page 36 for activities.

Then Ed was falling!
But Clunk was very fast. He moved one long metal arm.
'I have you,' said Clunk. 'You're going to be fine.'
Clunk started to carry Ed down to the ground.

When he saw Kelly, Ed said, 'I'm sorry. I'm never going to climb again!'

Ben was thinking.

'When the sun was shining on Clunk, the light bounced down to the ground,' he said. 'I have an idea. It might help with the shadow of the building on the park.'

He started to tell Kelly his idea.

Go to page 38 for activities.

Chapter Five

Ten months later, it was a beautiful spring afternoon. Grandpa and the children were walking to the little park again.

Rosie was holding Josh's hand. When she saw the two tall buildings, she smiled. 'I was right,' she said. 'They *are* beautiful!'

Kelly was waiting to meet them in the park with a picnic.

'Your buildings are fantastic!' said Grandpa. 'And the park isn't in the shadows now! It's nice and sunny!'

Kelly pointed to the second building. There were lots of mirrors on the side of it.

→ Go to page 40 for activities.

'I got the idea from Ben,' said Kelly. 'I gave the second building a new shape and we put special mirror glass on it. Now the sun's light bounces off the second building and down into the park. So there's no shadow from the first building!'

'And when the sun moves, the mirrors can move, too,' said Grandpa. 'The park's sunny all day!'

'Now it's a great place for a picnic!' said Rosie.

While they were eating, a young man walked across the park.

'Hello, Ed,' said Kelly. 'Please come and eat with us.'

Kelly smiled at Grandpa. 'When Ed leaves school, he wants to work for me. He wants to be an architect!'

'I'm going to make tall buildings!' said Ed.

Go to page 42 for activities.

Activities for pages 4–5

1 Match.

1 city
2 tall
3 build
4 summer
5 building
6 crane

2 Order the words.

1 beautiful / was / afternoon. / a / It / summer

It was a beautiful summer afternoon.

2 were / city. / in / Ben / the / Rosie and

____

3 go / wanted / park. / Josh / to / the / to

____

4 to / and / walked / the children / Grandpa / park. / the

____

5 new / People / working / a / were / building. / on

____

3 Look at the picture on page 4. Write *yes* or *no*.

1 Aunt Val is standing at the door. yes
2 Aunt Val is wearing a blue skirt. ______
3 The children are walking with Grandpa. ______
4 Josh is next to Ben and Clunk. ______
5 Ben has a ball. ______
6 Rosie has a bag. ______
7 There is a bird on a tree. ______

4 Complete the sentences.

building ~~go~~ walk is good pointed

1 Josh said, 'Can we go to the park?'
2 Josh ______ Ben and Rosie's little cousin.
3 They can ______ to the park in ten minutes.
4 Aunt Val told Josh to be ______.
5 Close to the park, Josh ______ to a crane.
6 A lot of people were ______ a tall building.

Talk **Do you like going to the park? What do you do at the park? Talk to a friend.**

Activities for pages 6–7

1 Write the words.

1 idea — d i e a

2 ____________ o h d a w s

3 ____________ n t e a m p t r a

4 ____________ e n d o s c

5 ____________ c i t c h a e r t

6 ____________ o c i f e f

2 Circle the correct words.

1 Kelly is **an** / **a** architect.

2 Kelly **was** / **had** the idea for the new building.

3 They **were** / **was** building a second building, too.

4 'Will they **making** / **make** a shadow on the park?'

Talk **What is a shadow? Talk to a friend.**

3 Choose and write the correct words.

A woman was [1] walking by the children, and heard Ben's [2] __________. 'This building is going to be offices and apartments,' she said. The [3] __________ was an architect and her name was Kelly. They were building a second [4] __________, too. 'Your buildings are going to be fantastic,' [5] __________ said. 'But will they make a shadow on the [6] __________?'

children

~~walking~~

building

Grandpa

Kelly

question

woman

park

Now tick (✓) the best name for Chapter One.

Offices around the park ☐

Apartments around the park ☐

Buildings around the park ☐

Activities for pages 8–9

1 Write the words.

climb ~~sun~~ slide down playground

1 sun ____________ 2 ____________ 3 ____________

4 ____________ 5 ____________

2 Look at pages 8 and 9. Complete the sentences. You can use 1, 2, or 3 words.

1 Josh was happy, but soon he was cold.
2 They were not in ____________ now.
3 It was cold in ____________ the new building.
4 They went ____________ playground.
5 A teenager was ____________ on the slide.
6 The boy's ____________ Ed.
7 Ed was too ____________ slide.

3 Choose the best answer.

1 Ben: Are you OK, Josh?

Josh: a No, I'm fine.

(b) No, I'm cold.

c No, I can't.

2 Ben: Do you want to go to the playground?

Josh: a Yes, please!

b Oh dear!

c Thank you!

3 Ben: Can you go down the slide?

Josh: a Yes, I am.

b Yes, I do.

c Yes, I can.

4 Ben: Oh dear, look at the slide.

Josh: a Oh, there are some big children.

b Oh, there are any big children.

c Oh, there are much big children.

5 Ben: That boy is too big for the slide.

Josh: a Yes, it is!

b Yes, he isn't!

c Yes, he is!

Activities for pages 10–11

1 Write the words.

1 s h o u t

2 _ _ _ _ _

3 _ _ _ _ _ _

4 _ _

2 Circle the correct answers.

1 What did Ed say about the playground?

it was angry (it was boring) it was good

2 Why did Josh want to go home?

he was cold and angry he was cold and tired

3 Who did they hear shouting?

Ed Clunk Kelly

4 Was Ed with his friends?

yes no

3 Choose and write the correct words.

Ed and [1] ___his___ friends left the playground, [2] ________ now Josh was cold and tired. He wanted [3] ________ home. Suddenly they heard an angry shout. It was Kelly! Ed's friends were there, but Ed [4] ________ with them. Kelly was [5] ________ up at the crane and shouting.

1 his he's him

4 didn't wasn't hadn't

2 for so but

5 looks looked looking

3 to go going go

4 Circle the odd one out.

1 angry / cold / play
2 cousin / home / friend
3 Ed / Kelly / Rosie
4 shout / climb / say

Talk **What do you think Ed was doing? Tell a friend your ideas.**

Activities for pages 12–13

1 Write the words.

1 __________ i h h g

2 __________ g u l a h

3 __________ d s e c r a

4 __________ o t p

2 Circle the mistakes. Then write the correct words.

1 Ed was climbing up the building. crane

2 Ed wasn't having fun. __________

3 Ed shouted down to his family. __________

4 Soon Ed was at the bottom of the crane. __________

5 Ed put up his legs and laughed. __________

6 But the crane was very top. __________

7 Now Ed was too happy to move. __________

3 Match. Then write the sentences.

1 Ed wasn't scared –	can climb anything!'
2 He shouted, 'I	at me up here!'
3 Ed went up to	he was having fun!
4 He shouted, 'Look	the top of the crane.

1 Ed wasn't scared – he was having fun!

2 ______

3 ______

4 ______

4 Look at the picture on page 12. Write *yes* or *no*.

1 Ed is climbing up the crane. ______

2 Ed is wearing blue jeans and a red sweatshirt. ______

3 The crane is yellow. ______

4 A woman is at the top of the crane. ______

5 Ben and Rosie are watching Ed. ______

6 There are some trees behind the crane. ______

7 Grandpa is next to Kelly. ______

Activities for pages 14–15

1 Choose and write the correct words.

a robot   heavy   a teenager   ~~the wind~~   strong

1 This is the name for air that moves. the wind

2 When something is difficult to carry. ______

3 This is made of metal, but can look like a person. ______

4 When a person can carry heavy things easily. ______

2 Match. Then complete the sentences.

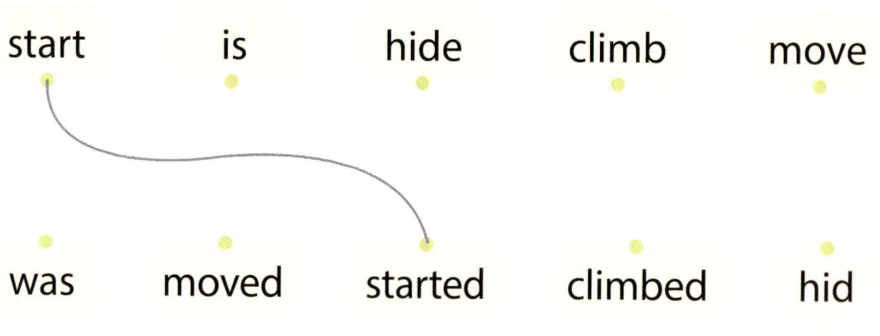

1 Clunk started to climb up the crane.

2 Clunk ______ up the crane fast.

3 He ______ across the arm of the crane.

4 Ed tried to ______ it, but he was scared.

5 The wind ______ getting stronger.

Talk **Can Clunk help Ed? Tell a friend your ideas.**

3 Who said this in Chapter Three? Write the names.

1 'I can go up there and bring him down.' Clunk

2 'HELP!' ______

3 'Look at me up here!' ______

4 'Be careful, Clunk!' ______

5 'I'm coming to help you.' ______

6 'Come down now! You might fall!' ______

4 Order the events in Chapter Three.

The wind started to get stronger. ______

Ed looked down and stopped laughing. ______

Kelly shouted, 'Come down now!' to Ed. ______

Ed climbed up the crane. 1

Clunk climbed up the crane. ______

Ed got to the top of the crane. ______

Clunk moved across the arm of the crane. ______

Now tick (✓) the best name for Chapter Three.

Clunk helps Ed ☐

Clunk finds Ed ☐

Clunk sees Ed ☐

Activities for pages 16–17

1 Match.

1 hold

2 shine

3 metal

4 ground

2 Circle the correct answers.

1 Where were Grandpa, Kelly, and the children?

on the crane   on the building   on the ground

2 What stopped Grandpa seeing Clunk?

the crane was in the way
the sun's light was hitting Clunk

3 What made Ed start to fall?

strong wind   Clunk's hand   Ben's shout

4 Did Ed fall to the ground?

yes   no

3 Order the words.

1 watching / The / were / and / children / waiting.

____

2 getting / Ed. / Clunk / closer / was / to

____

3 was / wind. / a very / Then / strong / there

____

4 the crane / one / holding / Ed / hand. / was / with

____

4 Look at pages 16 and 17. Complete the sentences. You can use 1, 2, or 3 words.

1 Rosie asked, '________________ OK?'

2 But Grandpa didn't ________________.

3 Clunk was at ________________ the crane.

4 He said, 'Give me ________________,' to Ed.

5 But Ed ________________ to fall.

6 Now Ed was ________________ with one hand.

7 Ed said, '________________ be quick!'

Talk **Can Clunk help Ed? Tell a friend your ideas.**

Activities for pages 18–19

1 Circle the mistakes. Then write the correct words.

1 Ed was falling, but Clunk was very slow. ______

2 Clunk moved his metal leg. ______

3 Clunk started to push Ed to the ground. ______

4 Ed said, 'I'm never going to run again!' ______

5 Rosie was thinking about the sun's light. ______

6 The sun's light bounced up to the ground. ______

7 Ben had an idea about the shadow of the crane. ______

2 Circle the correct words.

1 Clunk moved **him** / **his** long metal arm.

2 'You're going **to be** / **being** fine.'

3 When he saw Kelly, Ed said, '**I'm** / **I** sorry.'

4 Ed didn't want to **climbing** / **climb** again.

5 Ben had **the** / **an** idea.

6 Ben told Kelly **about** / **around** his idea.

3 Choose and write the correct words.

Clunk was at the top of the crane. He was getting [1] __________ to Ed, but suddenly there was a [2] __________ wind. Ed started to [3] __________. Now he was holding the [4] __________ with one hand. Ed was falling but Clunk was fast. He moved one long metal [5] __________ and carried Ed down to the [6] __________. Ed was very sorry and didn't want to climb again!

strong closer hand arm

ground fall climb crane

Now tick (✓) the best name for Chapter Four.

Thank you, Ed! ☐ Thank you, Clunk! ☐

Thank you, Kelly! ☐

Talk **What is Ben's idea? Tell a friend your ideas.**

Activities for pages 20–21

1 Choose and write the correct words.

Ten months [1] ________, Grandpa and the children went to the little park [2] ________. The two new buildings [3] ________ beautiful. Kelly was waiting for them. The buildings were fantastic and the park was nice and [4] ________. Kelly pointed to the second building. There were [5] ________ of mirrors on the side of it.

1 since more later

2 around about again

3 were was had

4 sun sunny sunnier

5 lots lot lot's

2 Match.

1 It was a beautiful	in the shadows now.
2 Kelly was in the	spring afternoon.
3 The park wasn't	park with a picnic.

3 Complete the sentences.

pointed holding waiting
smiled were walking

1 Grandpa and the children were ____________ to the park.
2 Rosie was ____________ Josh's hand.
3 When Rosie saw the buildings she ____________.
4 Kelly was ____________ for them in the park.
5 The buildings ____________ fantastic.
6 Kelly ____________ to the second building.

4 Look at the picture on page 21. Write *yes* or *no*.

1 There are two tall buildings around the park. ________
2 There are lots of trees in the park. ________
3 Kelly is sitting on the grass. ________
4 Kelly is wearing a green T-shirt. ________
5 Ben is walking next to Josh. ________
6 Josh is wearing green pants and red shoes. ________
7 Grandpa is talking to Clunk. ________
8 Ben is carrying a ball. ________

Activities for pages 22–23

1 Look at pages 22 and 23. Complete the sentences. You can use 1, 2, or 3 words.

1 Kelly ________________ from Ben.

2 The second building has a ________________ shape.

3 And it has ________________ on it.

4 Now the sun's light bounces down ________________ park.

5 A young ________________ walked across the park.

6 Ed wants to be ________________ when he leaves school.

7 He wants ________________ tall buildings!

2 Who said this? Write the names.

1 'Hello, Ed. Please come and eat with us.' ____________

2 'I got the idea from Ben.' ____________

3 'Now it's a great place for a picnic!' ____________

4 'I'm going to make tall buildings!' ____________

5 'So there's no shadow from the first building!' ____________

6 'The park's sunny all day!' ____________

3 Write the words from Chapter Five.

1 ____________ c e n o b u

2 ____________ r o r i m r

3 ____________ i n p c i c

4 ____________ i t f r s

5 ____________ s l s g a

6 ____________ g s r p i n

Now tick (✓) the best name for Chapter Five.

Amazing new buildings ☐

Amazing new parks ☐

Amazing new mirrors ☐

Talk **Do you like this story? Talk to a friend.**

Project

A New Building

Talk **Have you ever been in a tall building? Talk to a friend.**

1 Read about the Burj Khalifa.

Where is the Burj Khalifa?

It is in Dubai, in the United Arab Emirates.

How high is the Burj Khalifa?

The very top is 829.8 meters high.

When did people start building the Burj Khalifa?

They started building on January 6, 2004.

When did they finish building the Burj Khalifa?

They finished building on December 30, 2009.

When did the building open?

It opened on January 4, 2010.

What is special about the Burj Khalifa?

There are lots of special things about the Burj Khalifa. It has 163 floors, 24,348 windows, and the highest restaurant and swimming pool in the world!

Talk **Would you like to go to the top of the Burj Khalifa? Talk to a friend.**

2 Imagine you are an architect. Draw a new building. Then answer the questions about your building.

1 What is the name of your building? ____________

2 Where is your building? ____________

3 How high is your building? ____________

4 What is special about your building?

____

____

____

Picture Dictionary

angry

apartment

architect

boring

bounce

build

building

city

climb

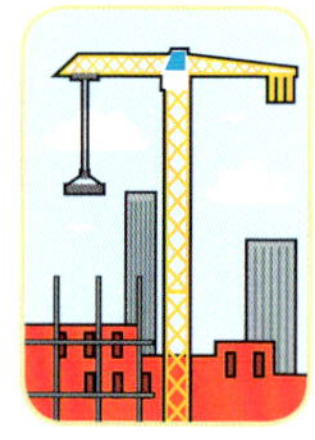
crane

down

first

glass

ground

heavy

high

hold

idea

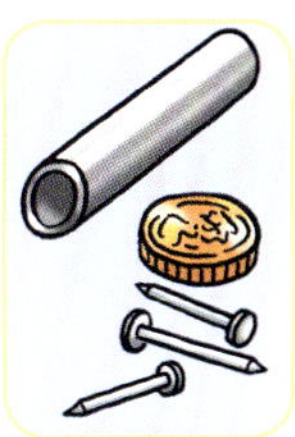
metal

mirror

office

picnic

second

shadow

shine (v)

slide (n)

spring

strong

summer

tall

teenager

up

Oxford Read and Imagine

Oxford Read and Imagine graded readers are at nine levels (Early Starter, Starter, Beginner, and Levels 1 to 6) for students from age 3 or 4 and older. They offer great stories to read and enjoy.

Activities provide Cambridge Young Learner Exams preparation. See Key below.

At Levels 1 to 6, every storybook reader links to an **Oxford Read and Discover** non-fiction reader, giving students a chance to find out more about the world around them, and an opportunity for Content and Language Integrated Learning (CLIL).

For more information about **Read and Imagine**, and for Teacher's Notes, go to www.oup.com/elt/teacher/readandimagine

KEY  Activity supports Cambridge Young Learners Movers Exam preparation

Oxford Read and Discover

Did you enjoy this story? Do you like buildings? Do you want to know how tall a skyscraper can be? To find out about super structures around the world, read this non-fiction book.

OXFORD
UNIVERSITY PRESS

Great Clarendon Street, Oxford, OX2 6DP, United Kingdom

Oxford University Press is a department of the University of Oxford. It furthers the University's objective of excellence in research, scholarship, and education by publishing worldwide. Oxford is a registered trade mark of Oxford University Press in the UK and in certain other countries

First published in 2016
2025
13

ISBN: 978 0 19 473674 9

Printed in China

This book is printed on paper from certified and well-managed sources

ACKNOWLEDGEMENTS

Main illustrations by: Matteo Piana.

Additional illustrations by: Dusan Pavlic/Beehive illustration; Alan Rowe; Mark Ruffle.

The Publishers would like to thank the following for their kind permission to reproduce photographs and other copyright material: Shutterstock p.44.